Date: 2/27/13

Teachers Help Us

Aaron R. Murray

Enslow Elementary

an imprint of

Enslow Publishers, Inc.

40 Industrial Road
Box 398
Berkeley Heights, NJ 07922
USA

http://www.enslow.com

Enslow Elementary, an imprint of Enslow Publishers, Inc.
Enslow Elementary® is a registered trademark of Enslow Publishers, Inc.

Library of Congress Cataloging-in-Publication Data
Murray, Aaron R.
 Teachers help us / Aaron R. Murray.
    p. cm. — (All about community helpers)
 Includes index.
 Summary: "Introduces pre-readers to simple concepts about what teachers do using short sentences
and repetition of words"—Provided by publisher.
  ISBN 978-0-7660-4045-8
 1. Teachers—Juvenile literature. I. Title.
 LB1775.M815 2013
 371.1—dc23   2011031048

Future editions:
Paperback ISBN 978-1-4644-0055-1
ePUB ISBN 978-1-4645-0962-9
PDF ISBNs 978-1-4646-0962-6

Printed in the United States of America
032012 Lake Book Manufacturing, Inc., Melrose Park, IL
10 9 8 7 6 5 4 3 2 1

To Our Readers: We have done our best to make sure all Internet Addresses in this book were active
and appropriate when we went to press. However, the author and the publisher have no control over and
assume no liability for the material available on those Internet sites or on other Web sites they may link
to. Any comments or suggestions can be sent by e-mail to comments@enslow.com or to the address on
the back cover.

♻ Enslow Publishers, Inc., is committed to printing our books on recycled paper. The paper in every
book contains 10% to 30% post-consumer waste (PCW). The cover board on the outside of each book
contains 100% PCW. Our goal is to do our part to help young people and the environment too!

Photo Credits: © 2011 Photos.com, a division of Getty Images, pp. 14, 22; iStockphoto.
com: © Agnieszka Kirinicjanow, p. 18, © Chris Schmidt, p. 6 (bottom left), © Christopher
Futcher, pp. 12—13, © Loretta Hostettler, p. 6 (bottom right), © RonTech2000, p. 8;
Shutterstock.com, pp. 1, 3 (classroom, science), 4, 6 (top), 10, 16, 20; Shutterstock.com:
Nadejda Ivanova, p. 3 (history).

Cover Photo: © 2011 Photos.com, a division of Getty Images

Note to Parents and Teachers
Help pre-readers get a jump-start on reading. These lively stories introduce simple concepts with
repetition of words and short, simple sentences. Photos and illustrations fill the pages with color and
effectively enhance the text. Free Educator Guides are available for this series at www.enslow.com.
Search for the *All About Community Helpers* series name.

Contents

Words to Know

classroom   history   science

Teachers work
in schools.

They help people
learn new things.

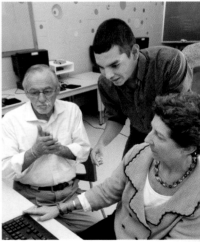

Some teach
young kids.

Some teach
older kids.

Some teach
grown-ups.

You have
teachers too.

Teachers help
you learn science.

They also help you
learn math and
history.

Some teach music or art.

13

Some teach gym.

Teachers can work in classrooms.

Teachers can also work outside.

Teachers help
people learn
many new things.

Do you like teaching people? You may want to be a teacher.

Read More

Deedrick, Tami. *Teachers*. Mankato, Minn.: Capstone Press, 2006.

Mitchell, Melanie. *Teachers*. Minneapolis, Minn.: Lerner Classroom, 2004.

Vogel, Elizabeth. *Meet My Teacher.* New York: PowerKids Press, 2002.

Web Sites

Enchanted Learning. *Community Helpers Activity Book.* <http://www.enchantedlearning.com/books/communityhelpers/activity>

Index

Guided Reading Level: C
Guided Reading Leveling System is based on the guidelines recommended by Fountas and Pinnell.

Word Count: 74